I Pray Like Jesus!

Written by Josep Codina
Illustrated by Roser Rius

PRAYING WITH LITTLE ONES

Pauline
BOOKS & MEDIA

Jesus spent a lot of time talking with his friends.
He liked being with them!

Jesus' friends watched what Jesus did.
Jesus' friends listened to what he said.
Jesus' friends learned how to love
as Jesus did.

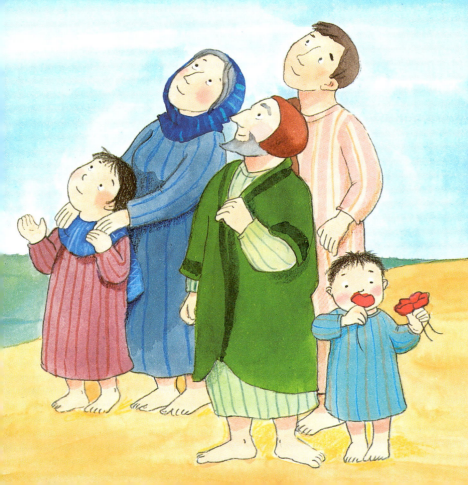

Sometimes, Jesus would go off
by himself to a quiet place.

"What is he doing over there?"
said his friends. "Let's go and ask him."

"Why do you want to be alone, Jesus?"
his friends asked.

"I want to speak with my Heavenly
Father," Jesus said. "I am praying."

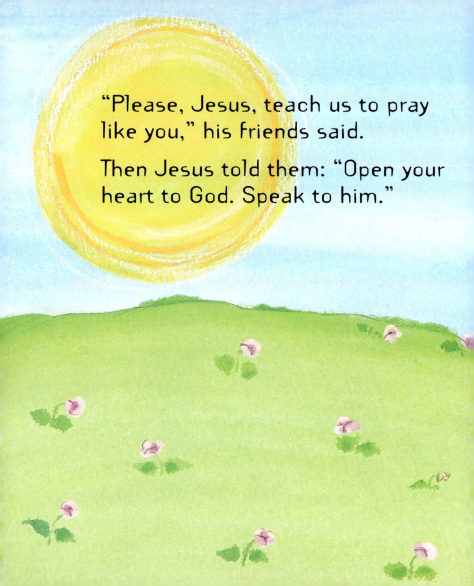

And Jesus taught this prayer to his friends:

OUR FATHER,
WHO ART IN HEAVEN,

HALLOWED BE THY NAME.
THY KINGDOM COME.

THY WILL BE DONE ON EARTH AS IT IS IN HEAVEN.

GIVE US THIS DAY OUR DAILY BREAD,

AND FORGIVE US OUR
TRESPASSES
AS WE FORGIVE THOSE
WHO TRESPASS AGAINST US.

AND LEAD US NOT
INTO TEMPTATION,
BUT DELIVER US FROM EVIL.
AMEN.

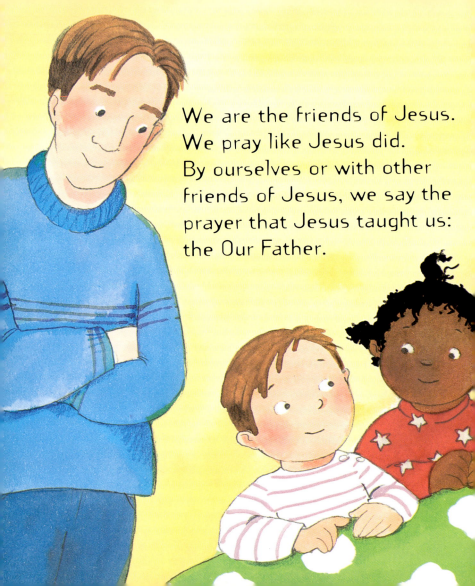

We are the friends of Jesus. We pray like Jesus did. By ourselves or with other friends of Jesus, we say the prayer that Jesus taught us: the Our Father.

To Parents and Teachers

Every child wants to behave like an adult. He or she admires adults and tries to imitate them.

This third book of the Praying with Little Ones Series leads children to open their hearts to our Heavenly Father as Jesus did. It invites them to begin to learn and to pray the Our Father.

More than simply teaching our children prayers, it is very important that we adults actually pray together with them—at home, in school and in church. In this way we will nurture their desire for God and initiate them into the Christian community's life of prayer.

Pauline Books and Media Centers operated by the Daughters of St. Paul:

3908 Sepulveda Blvd., Culver City, CA 90230 310-397-8676

5945 Balboa Ave., San Diego, CA 92111 858-565-9181

46 Geary St., San Francisco, CA 94108 415-781-5180

145 SW 107th Ave., Miami, FL 33174 305-559-6715

1143 Bishop St., Honolulu, HI 96813 808-521-2731

For Neighbor Islands: 800-259-8463

172 N. Michigan Ave., Chicago, IL 60601 312-346-4228

4403 Veterans Blvd., Metairie, LA 70006 504-887-7631

Rt 1, 885 Providence Hwy., Dedham, MA 02026 781-326-5385

9804 Watson Rd., St. Louis, MO 63126 314-965-3512

561 US Rt. 1, Wick Plaza, Edison, NJ 08817 732-572-1200

150 E. 52nd St., New York, NY 10022 212-754-1110

2105 Ontario St., Cleveland, OH 44115 216-621-9427

9171-A Roosevelt Blvd., Philadelphia, PA 19114 215-676-9494

243 King St., Charleston, SC 29401 843-577-0175

4811 Poplar Ave., Memphis, TN 38117 901-761-2987

114 Main Plaza, San Antonio, TX 78205 210-224-8101

1025 King St., Alexandria, VA 22314 703-549-3806

3022 Dufferin St., Toronto, Ontario, Canada M6B 3T5 416-781-9131

1155 Yonge St., Toronto, Ontario, Canada M4T 1W2 416-934-3440

Original title: *Prego com Jesús!*

English adaptation by Patricia Edward Jablonski, FSP

Copyright © 2002, Editorial Claret, S.A.
Barcelona, Spain (World Rights)

ISBN 0-8198-3684-2

Published in the U.S.A. by Pauline Books & Media,
50 Saint Pauls Avenue, Boston, MA 02130-3491.

Printed in Spain.

www.pauline.org

Pauline Books & Media is the publishing house of
the Daughters of St. Paul, an international congregation
of women religious serving the Church with the communications media.

1 2 3 4 5   06 05 04 03 02